The
Whole Person
Leader

Unlock your potential to inspire, influence, and lead with purpose

By David Hatzfeld

INTUITION
EXISTS

First Edition: 2025

Written by David Hatzfeld
Edited By Kristen Hatzfeld
Cover design by: H Khan
Published by Intuition Exists LLC
ISBN: 9798999095510
Printed in the United States of America

This book is designed for personal growth and leadership development and offers a companion workbook. For bulk orders, corporate licensing, or workshop permissions, please contact:

Intuition Exists
info@intuitionexists.com

This book is dedicated to my beautiful wife who is my inspiration. She makes me want to be the best man I can be every day.

Acknowledgment

Writing this book has been a journey of growth, reflection, and purpose—and I could not have done it alone.

To my incredible spouse and family: thank you for your unwavering support, your patience during late nights and early mornings, and your belief in this message. Your love has been my anchor.

To Jack, Joe, Sam, Lily, Kayla, and Hunter; you inspire me to grow as a leader and a father.

To the mentors, coaches, and leaders who have poured wisdom into me over the years — your guidance shaped both my leadership and my life. I'm grateful for every lesson, every challenge, and every opportunity to grow under your influence.

To my friends and early readers who offered encouragement, feedback, and inspiration along the way—thank you for reminding me of the power of words and the importance of this work.

To every leader striving to make a difference in their homes, workplaces, and communities—this book is for you. May it equip and empower you to lead with authenticity, purpose, and heart.

And above all, I thank God for the calling, the courage, and the clarity to bring this book to life.

Table of Contents

Introduction

Do you want to be a more effective leader — whether in the workplace, at home, or in your community? Leadership isn't confined to titles, corner offices, or business suits. It's about influence, integrity, and impact. It's about becoming the kind of person others naturally want to follow — because of who you are, not just what you do.

Leading the Whole Person means acknowledging and understanding the full humanity of those you lead — not just their skills, roles, or output, but their emotions, values, aspirations, and personal challenges. It requires seeing people as more than employees or team members; they are individuals with stories, strengths, and struggles. Whole Person Leadership calls us to lead with empathy, curiosity, and respect, recognizing that when we honor the human value in others, we unlock their greatest potential. True leadership doesn't just move projects forward—it moves people forward.

This book will teach you how to become a Whole Person Leader — a leader who leads not just with skills, but with heart, character, and clarity. You'll learn how to grow in self-awareness, lead through purpose, and cultivate influence that drives meaningful, lasting success. Whether you're a seasoned executive, a new manager, a parent, or someone simply wanting to make a greater difference, the tools in these pages are designed to elevate your leadership from the inside out.

Grab life by the horns. Lead with purpose. And start creating the impact you were meant to make.

Chapter 1.

The Foundation: The Power of ACE

Many years ago, when my oldest son was in elementary school, he came home with his head hanging low. His best friend had suddenly decided they weren't friends anymore. No explanation. Just distance. And for a young boy, that kind of rejection cuts deep. He was heartbroken, confused, and discouraged.

I sat with him and gently asked what had happened. He shrugged. He didn't know. There was no big fight, no obvious reason — just the sting of being left out. I told him something that I hoped he would carry with him for life: "You can't control how other people act, but you can always control how you respond. You can choose to be your best self, even when others don't."

That day, we talked about the three things in life we always have full control over — no matter the situation: Attitude, Character, and Effort.

Those three things spell ACE. In every context, an ACE represents excellence. It's the highest card in the deck, the top fighter pilot in the squadron, or an unstoppable serve in tennis. No matter how it is used, ACE represents the best.

When you operate with ACE—when you lead with the right attitude, uphold strong character, and give your best effort— you're showing up as the best version of yourself. And that's what leadership is all about.

Attitude

Attitude is the bedrock of ACE and leadership. If your attitude goes unchecked, running wild and fancy-free then everything around you will crumble and fall. You will be perceived as irrational with your attitude all over the place. You must take your attitude captive because you alone can control it. When was the last time you had a toxic attitude? Did the situation improve or worsen? Were you endearing or repulsive? Attitudes are contagious — especially in leadership. The way you carry yourself sets the tone for everyone on your team. You can be frustrated and still lead with composure. You can feel pressure and still respond with clarity.

Controlling your attitude doesn't mean pretending to be cheerful all the time — it means choosing the mindset that best serves the moment. Leadership is about showing up with emotional discipline, even when the situation isn't ideal. That's what makes your attitude powerful.

Early in my career, I operated the largest sports bar in America located in Tulsa, OK. When the University of Oklahoma played Florida State in the College Football National Championship game, my venue was named the official watch party center. Within an hour before the kick-off, we reached our capacity of 2000. The Fire Marshal stood in front of our doors like a bouncer. I stepped into the kitchen just to make a quick check — then suddenly, the order ticket machine lit up like a slot machine on Jackpot. Every table had ordered food all at once. The staff froze in panic. Eyes darted to me. What now?

I was panicking inside too — In the chaos, I thought of something a mentor once told me: "It's hard to remember your job is to drain the swamp when you're up to your neck in alligators."

So I remembered my job. Leadership is about how you respond. In this scenario, I organized the team into stations to facilitate the orders more efficiently. I told the waitstaff on the floor to only do drink orders until we could catch up. Within an hour we were back in rhythm.

It took a determined attitude to keep moving forward and stay focused. As we powered through the night at breakneck speed, I stepped in wherever I could—but more than anything, I made it a point to offer genuine encouragement and praise.

Never underestimate the impact of sincere, well-timed praise. It's more than just kind words —it's fuel for morale, a signal that someone's effort is seen, and a powerful motivator that often unlocks another level of performance. Praise, when it's authentic and specific, reminds people that their contribution matters. In moments of pressure or fatigue, it can be the one thing that helps a teammate push a little harder, stay a little longer, or believe a little more in what they're doing.

It costs you nothing to genuinely praise, but the dividends it pays you back are huge. It is the greatest leadership investment you can make in your team. Not only does it lift up the recipient of the praise, but it has ripple effects across the team. As Ronald Reagan famously said, "A hide tide floats all ships." Your praises and encouragement are that high tide for your team.

We had the single biggest revenue day in our facility's history. We also received over 500 five-star Yelp reviews from that night. It could have been a disaster, but the attitude of the leader changed it to success.

In any high-pressure moment, people will follow your tone before they follow your instructions. So lead with composure, focus, and praise—and watch your team rise to meet you.

Character

It is often said that the most authentic version of you is what you show when no one else is watching. Only you can decide to do the right thing; to live a life of integrity. You have sole control over doing the right things all the time. As a leader, those whom you lead will follow your example. They will do what you do and what you expect.

In one of my favorite movies, *Cinderella Man,* James J Braddock (Played by Russell Crowe) discovers his oldest son stole a salami from the local butcher. The boy did not steal from greed. It was the Great Depression and his family was hurting. He had heard that children of a neighboring family were sent away because their parents couldn't feed them anymore. The boy desperately wanted to keep his family together and did not want to risk being separated possibly for good from the parents he loved. He was driven by what most people would say is a noble cause. James Braddock walked back to the butcher with his son and made his son hand back the salami and apologize. On the way back, he told his son that we don't steal ever. He promised they would never be split up as a family. When he could not fulfill this promise, James Braddock went to the state of New York for aid. This was prior to welfare or other state benefits that exist today. With the money he received, he brought his children back home. James Braddock demonstrated the art of character in so many ways, but the most profound was when he paid the state back every penny he received.

Doing the right thing and upholding integrity is what we do. This should be a part of the culture you are establishing. Those whom you lead will look to you as the ethical leader and will model the integrity they see in you.

Effort

Only you can decide whether you're going to work hard — or hardly work. It's easy to just go through the motions. Too often, leaders coast on autopilot, reacting instead of leading. But true leadership requires intentionality. I call it *living life on purpose.*

After college, I had the privilege of playing professional lacrosse—a dream come true. But the title "professional" wasn't just about talent; it was about discipline. Every single day was designed with purpose.

I had a strength coach who tailored workouts to make me stronger. A speed coach who planned drills to make me faster. An agility coach who trained me to move with precision. And a dietician who built a nutrition plan to fuel every ounce of my performance. Nothing was left to chance. Every detail was deliberate. That's what separates amateurs from professionals: intentional effort, every single day.

The same applies to leadership. If you want to be exceptional—not just present—you must lead on purpose. Show up each day with a plan, a goal, and a commitment to excellence. Leadership, like elite athletics, isn't accidental. It's built on daily, purposeful decisions that move you and your team forward.

As a leader, you're responsible for guiding your team across multiple critical initiatives. Without a clear, actionable daily plan for each one, you risk falling short of your full potential—and so does your team. Excellence doesn't happen by accident. Lead with intention. Live life on purpose!

The Power of ACE

As you begin to take control of your attitudes, something powerful starts to happen—you stop reacting to life and begin responding with intention. This shift may seem subtle at first, but it creates a ripple effect in every area of your life. When you commit to a life of integrity—where your values align with your words and actions—you establish a deep sense of trust, both in yourself and in the eyes of those you lead. And when you live life on purpose, not just by routine or reaction, your decisions carry clarity, your influence grows, and your relationships deepen.

These internal choices form the core of who you are as a leader. This is the foundation upon which all authentic and sustainable leadership is built. Leadership is not about titles or tasks — it's about who you are when no one's watching and how you show up when it matters most.

Now that we've laid this foundation, it's time to explore a powerful framework to guide your growth: ACE—Attitude, Character, and Effort. These three elements will serve as your compass as you continue to develop as a Whole Person Leader. In the next section, we'll unpack each one and show you how to actively apply them in your daily life and leadership journey.

Chapter 2.

The Whole Person Leader

In the evolving landscape of leadership, the demand is no longer just for competent managers or visionary strategists. Today's world calls for a Whole Person Leader — these are leaders who lead not only with their mind, but also with their heart, their values, and a deep sense of self- awareness, and awareness of the needs of those whom we serve. Whole Person leaders bring their full humanity to the table as they wear the multiple hats of leadership when interacting with associates. Whole Person leaders leverage their experience and resources to help associates become the best version of themselves they can be. They integrate personal growth with professional excellence which creates an environment for others to do the same.

Defining the Whole Person Leader

A Whole Person Leader understands that leadership isn't limited to tasks, goals, or performance metrics. It means leading people in all their complexity—acknowledging that they bring their full selves to work, with personal challenges, emotional burdens, and real-life struggles. Because people are not one-dimensional, leadership shouldn't be either.

Effective leadership begins with creating an environment where people feel safe — safe to speak up, to be honest, and even to be vulnerable. When that kind of trust exists, your team members know they can bring uncertainties to you without fear of judgment or dismissal.

Years ago, one of my top performers started coming in late without explanation. It was completely out of character, and I had every reason to be frustrated. I could've simply reminded her of our policies and demanded improvement. But instead, I chose to lead with compassionate curiosity. I didn't say, "What's going on?"—which can sound confrontational. I asked, "Is everything okay?"

That simple shift opened the door to a meaningful conversation. She broke down in tears and explained that her daughter was being severely bullied at school. She was exhausted, overwhelmed, and unsure of how to help her child. She apologized for sharing something so personal, but I assured her she wasn't alone.

As a parent of six and a former youth leader, I had been through similar struggles and was able to listen, empathize, and offer perspective. More importantly, I pointed her toward company resources she hadn't known existed—mental health support, counseling services, and more. Just by being present and informed, I helped her navigate a painful time — and, in turn, helped her feel seen, valued, and supported.

That's Whole Person Leadership in action.

It's about showing up not just as a manager, but as a human being. It's about leading both professionally and personally — offering guidance, support, and empathy when it matters most. This 360-degree approach to leadership builds trust that goes far deeper than titles or roles. It creates a culture rooted in care, empowerment, and meaningful connection.

A Whole Person Leader acknowledges and embraces the full spectrum of the human experience—mental, emotional, physical, and even spiritual. Rather than compartmentalizing life into "work" and "personal," they lead with integrity and authenticity across all spheres. Because when people know they can bring their whole selves to work, they're more engaged, more loyal, and more likely to thrive.

Whole Person Leaders are:

- **Highly Self-Aware** — They continuously reflect on their motivations, behaviors, perspectives and the impact they have in leadership environments.

- **Emotionally Intelligent** — They are empathetic, attuned to the needs of others, and highly skilled in managing interpersonal relationships.

- **Ethically Grounded** — Guided by values and principles, especially when decisions are difficult.

- **Holistically Healthy** — Attentive to their own physical, mental and emotional well-being.

- **Relationally Connected** — Committed to building trust and fostering meaningful collaboration

The Four Dimensions of Whole Person Leadership

1. **Intellectual Dimension: Leading with Clarity and Vision**

   The Whole Person Leader uses their intellect not just to analyze and strategize, but to envision possibilities and inspire greatness. They are committed to lifelong learning and nurture a growth mindset, not just in themselves, but in those they lead.

They should focus on:

- Clarity of purpose — Where are we going?

- Strategic thinking — How are we going to get there?

- Adapt and learn — What tactical changes need to happen to get us there?

2. **Emotional Dimension: Leading with Empathy and Presence**

Leadership is deeply relational. Whole Person Leaders excel in emotional intelligence. They know themselves, regulate their emotions, balance emotion and logic effectively, and deeply understand others. This emotional presence creates psychological safety and encourages open, honest dialogue.

Whole Person Leaders show empathy and actively listen. They demonstrate authenticity and appropriate vulnerability. They manage conflict effectively and constructively.

3. **Physical Dimension: Leading with Energy and Vitality**

Health and well-being are not luxuries; they are *leadership essentials*. A Whole Person Leader takes health and well-being seriously. By prioritizing physical health, they lead by example and motivate others to pursue greater balance in their own lives. Physical energy underpins stamina, focus, and resilience.

To sustain effective work habits, one must focus on well-being in order to go the distance and achieve the goal. Whole Person Leaders demonstrate healthy work/life balance always carving out time for self-care and critical personal relationships. Finally, Whole Person Leaders encourage and champion the well-being of others.

4. **Moral and Spiritual Dimension—Leading with Integrity and Purpose**

Without vision, the people will fail. This is a commonly repeated quotation, but it does not tell the whole story. *Whole Person Leaders must be intentional.* You need to do life on purpose. Too many people are just floating through life without any idea what they are doing or where they are going. This should NEVER be the case in leadership. Whole Person Leaders have a vision that is highly communicated and a direction on how to get there.

Whole Person Leadership is anchored in the values of the leader. They understand the 'Why' of the vision and their own personal 'Why'.

Leaders are servants, which may seem paradoxical, but effective leaders are servants. The goal of leadership should be to help others to become the best version of themselves that they can be. Effective leaders facilitate that transformation in others. This is a purpose-driven approach to leading. It requires the leader to *really* get to know those they lead so they can understand how to help them become the best version of themselves. This is how championship teams are created.

Whole Person Leaders are highly ethical. They do the right things the right way all of the time. They uphold a standard of excellence with a mantra, "We do it the right way or we don't do it at all."

The ethical tone is set by the leader. Those whom you lead will do what you allow. Leadership is not only about setting goals or driving performance — it's about establishing the moral compass for the entire team or organization. A leader's values, behaviors, and boundaries create the ethical climate in which others operate. If you, as a leader, tolerate dishonesty, corner-cutting, disrespect, or a lack of accountability, you send a clear message—whether spoken or not—that such behavior is acceptable.

People look to leaders for cues on what is permissible. Even in high-pressure environments, where the temptation to compromise may arise, the leader's integrity becomes the standard. If you consistently model honesty, fairness, and responsibility, your team will follow suit. Conversely, if you remain silent in the face of misconduct or turn a blind eye to unethical choices, you've essentially granted permission through your inaction.

Leadership is influence, and that influence is amplified when it comes to ethics. You don't just lead through what you say — you lead through what you tolerate. The question is not just what kind of leader do you want to be, but also what kind of culture are you willing to allow?

Impact of the Whole Person Leader

Organizations that are led by Whole Person Leaders thrive by having inclusive and supportive environments. These organizations benefit from increased engagement. People feel seen, valued and inspired. When your goal is to help people become the best version of themselves that they can be, then they feel empowered through your inspiration and encouragement.

The Whole Person Leader creates stronger cultures of trust, inclusion and authenticity. This culture not only retains employees but also attracts top talent. Culture is the defining trademark of The Whole Person Leader.

By creating an inspiring culture, the company led by Whole Person Leaders are better equipped to weather the economic storms of change. Because of the vision cast by The Whole Person Leader, those companies are more agile and fluid. They are empowered with courage to tackle the ever-changing industrial environment.

Finally, The Whole Person Leader creates sustainable success, because the leader focuses on long-term human flourishing and not short-term metrics.

How to become a Whole Person Leader

Being a Whole Person Leader is not a destination; it is a journey. Leadership isn't about getting results or climbing the ladder. These are biproducts of being a Whole Person Leader. It is not about showing up, it's about being fully engaged, intentional and in the present. You are not a "boss" or "decision maker," you are a servant leader. You are facilitating transformation. In today's world, the leaders that make the biggest impact aren't necessarily the smartest, the most resourceful, the most connected, or the leader with the title. The biggest impact is made by leaders that lead with humility, intention, integrity, and wholeness.

That is what it means to be a Whole Person Leader. You don't check parts of yourself at the door when you walk into a meeting. Whole Person Leaders lead with both their head and their heart. You honor your values. You pay attention to your energy, your mindset and your relationships.

Chapter 3.

The Humble Leader

Leadership is often imagined as a forceful climb to the top — a role marked by authority, confidence, and charisma. Yet the most transformative leaders throughout history have often been the most humble. Humility, contrary to being a sign of weakness, is a quiet strength that inspires trust, cultivates loyalty, and fosters growth within teams. Being a humble leader is not about shrinking back — it is about stepping forward with self-awareness, openness, and a genuine respect for others. Humility is an essential characteristic of the Whole Person Leader.

The Essence of Humble Leadership

Humble leaders lead with the mindset that leadership is not about them — it's about the people they serve. They understand that their position is not a badge of superiority, but a responsibility to elevate others. These leaders recognize their own limitations and invite others to fill the gaps. They seek input, listen deeply, and celebrate team wins over personal accolades.

This kind of leadership doesn't shout. It resonates. It attracts. It is desired.

Why Humility Matters

In a world that often rewards ego and visibility, humility might seem counterintuitive. But the data and stories tell a different tale. Humble leaders create psychologically safe environments where team members feel free to speak up, take risks, and innovate. They are more approachable and more trusted.

Humble leaders build stronger cultures — because people follow leaders who respect them, not just those who direct them.

The Traits of a Humble Leader

1. Self-Awareness: Humble leaders have a clear view of their strengths and weaknesses. They own their mistakes and are open to feedback.

2. Empathy: They genuinely care about their team's well-being and success.

3. Gratitude: They give credit generously and acknowledge the contributions of others.

4. Openness: They are willing to learn from anyone—regardless of title or experience.

5. Service: They lead from a place of service, always asking, "How can I help?"

Leading Without the Ego

Humility doesn't mean a lack of confidence. It means having the confidence to put the mission and the team above personal pride. It's the ability to say, "I was wrong," or "You were right," without fear of losing authority. It's knowing when to step back so others can shine.

Great leaders don't need to be the smartest in the room — they just need to bring out the best in those who are.

How to Practice Humble Leadership

- Listen more than you speak. Create space for others to contribute.

- Admit when you don't know something. It builds credibility and models lifelong learning.

- Ask for feedback. And more importantly, act on it.

- Elevate others. Give recognition publicly and consistently.

- Lead by example. Demonstrate integrity, honesty, and humility in your daily actions.

The Legacy of Humility

Humble leadership leaves a lasting impact. It doesn't just drive performance — it builds people. It teaches others how to lead with heart, resilience, and authenticity. When leaders lead with humility, they give others the courage to lead the same way. That's how movements are born, cultures are shaped, and lives are changed.

As Jim Collins wrote in *Good to Great*, the most effective leaders blend "personal humility with professional will." They are fiercely committed to the mission — but without needing the spotlight.

And that is the paradox of humble leadership: when you let go of the need to be seen, you become the kind of leader everyone remembers and wants to follow.

It seems counterintuitive in a world that rewards visibility, charisma, and self-promotion. But the truth is, the most unforgettable leaders are not the ones constantly stepping into the spotlight —they're the ones quietly shining it on others. They don't lead to be admired; they lead to make a difference. And in doing so, they earn a deeper, more lasting kind of influence.

Humble leaders don't need to be the loudest voice in the room. Their presence is felt in their consistency, their kindness, their integrity. They empower others, build trust, and take responsibility. Over time, these qualities leave an impression that outlasts any speech or spotlight. People follow them not because they're impressed—but because they're inspired.

This is the paradox: when you stop trying to be significant, you become significant. When you lead for others, not for applause, your impact multiplies. The very act of surrendering the ego makes room for your leadership to take root in the hearts of others.

Humble Leaders may not always be seen,
but they are never forgotten.

Chapter 4.

Having a Let's Go Attitude

The "Let's Go" Attitude is Leading with Energy, Belief, and Urgency. Every great team, bold mission, or breakthrough moment begins with a spark. Not a perfectly written plan. Not a unanimous vote. But a surge of belief—someone saying, "Let's go." That phrase is more than motivation. It's a mindset. A rallying cry. A leadership posture that turns uncertainty into action, and inertia into momentum.

The "Let's Go" attitude doesn't wait for conditions to be perfect. It trusts the process, embraces the challenge, and leads forward—because forward is where the future lives.

After entering the world of sales, I was preparing to land a really big account that potentially could have been the biggest deal of my year. As I talked through the nuances of the case with my mentor, he noticed that there were threads of doubt in my tone. When he pulled it out of me asking what the issue was, I said "What if they say no?" He just looked at me and then smiled. I was a little taken aback by the fact that he was being so nonchalant in the midst of my doubts. Then he said something so profound it changed my life forever. He said, "What's the worst that can happen? Will he kick you out and call the police? Will he curse you out? Will he humiliate you? Of course not, don't you realize you are already at No, it can only go up from here."

You wake up already at No. This is huge freedom because it allows you to take risks, it allows you to try anything. You are already at No; it can only get better.

What is the "Let's Go" Attitude?

The "Let's Go" attitude is a contagious blend of positivity, courage, and decisive energy. It's the belief that something meaningful can be built from where we are, with what we have. It's not blind optimism or reckless speed. It's grounded urgency — a refusal to stall out in fear or overthinking.

Whole Person Leaders embrace the let's go mentality and inspire confidence to venture forth. They inspire action. remove hesitation and unlock potential by modeling enthusiasm and resolve. When a team hears "Let's go" from their leader, they don't just hear words—they feel momentum. It becomes a "we can do it" mentality.

The Power Behind "Let's Go"

1   Momentum is Magic: Action creates clarity. Even small steps in motion create energy and reveal the next path forward. It is essential to get early wins.

2   People Follow Energy: Teams take cues from their leaders. A "Let's Go" leader lifts spirits, raises standards, and makes people want to move.

3   Breaks Through Fear: Fear thrives in stillness. The "Let's Go" attitude is a choice to act in spite of uncertainty.

4   Builds Resilience: This mindset says, "We'll figure it out as we go." It makes teams adaptable and resourceful, not paralyzed by imperfection.

Traits of a "Let's Go" Leader

- Decisive: Not impulsive, but bold enough to make a call and commit to it.

- Optimistic: Looks for possibilities, not just problems.

- Encouraging: Inspires confidence and helps others see what they're capable of.

- Action-Oriented: Focuses on execution over endless planning.

- Resilient: When knocked down, gets up quickly and says, "Let's go again."

Shifting Into "Let's Go" Mode

You don't have to feel ready to lead with energy. You choose it.

- Start with belief. Believe in the mission, your people, and the process.

- Speak it. Language matters. Say, "Let's go," and mean it. Let your words move people.

- Simplify the next step. Clear action beats complex plans.

- Model urgency. Show up with energy. Walk with purpose. Respond quickly.

- Celebrate progress. Every win builds momentum.

When "Let's Go" Meets Resistance

You'll face hesitation — from yourself or your team. That's normal. The antidote isn't pressure — it's clarity and courage.

Remind your team what's possible. Connect the mission to meaning. Help them see the win on the other side of the risk.

Growth invites uncertainty, and progress often begins with discomfort. Clarity gives direction. Courage gives momentum. As a leader, it's your job to bring both. When doubt creeps in, remind your team — and yourself — what's possible. Reconnect everyone to the "why" behind the work. Don't just talk about the mission; make it meaningful. Show how it matters, how it changes lives, how it moves people forward. Possibility lives on the other side of fear — your job is to help them see it.

Trust isn't built through performance. It's built through presence. And belief isn't built in a single moment — it's built every day you show up, live the mission, and lead with heart.

And don't fake hype — live it. Your authenticity fuels trust. Your consistency builds belief.

Living the "Let's Go" Life

This attitude isn't just for projects or peak moments. It's a lifestyle of showing up with intention, energy, and a readiness to act. It's walking into the room and bringing hope. It's raising your hand when others hesitate. It's choosing movement over fear and belief over doubt. You are the Captain of the ship. As Lt Colonel Hal Moore said, "I will be the first onto the battlefield and I will be the last off of it." He was a "Let's Go" leader demonstrating a willingness to take the first step of risk. With him leading the charge, every soldier behind him had the confidence to follow, knowing they were going somewhere.

Two simple words — yet they carry the spark that ignites movements, launches visions, and builds dreams. Not eventually. Not someday. But now.

Whether you're leading a team into uncharted territory, standing at the edge of a new opportunity, or simply trying to face a Monday morning with purpose — remember this: momentum doesn't wait for permission. It begins the moment someone stands up and says, "Let's go". It's more than a phrase. It's a mindset. It's a decision to move, to lead, to believe that what lies ahead is worth the risk. It's the battle cry of the dreamer, the leader, the builder — the person who understands that growth doesn't happen in comfort zones.

Be open to the idea that the next breakthrough might not come from a grand plan at all. As a leader, visionary, or dreamer — your job isn't to predict every detail. It's to stay open, stay ready, and stay in motion. Because sometimes, the shift that changes everything begins with one unplanned, undeniable "Let's go."

Chapter 5.

Success Is Built On The Path Of Failure

In a world that often glorifies overnight success, it is easy to overlook the stumbles, setbacks, and silent struggles that pave the way to greatness. Failure is not the opposite of success —it is the foundation. Every great achievement is built upon a series of missteps that shaped the individual, sharpened their resolve, and taught them lessons that triumph alone never could. To understand success, one must first understand the indispensable role of failure in the journey.

The Misunderstood Teacher

Failure, though often feared, is one of life's most powerful teachers. It strips away illusion and forces a confrontation with reality. When we fail, we are forced to examine our methods, question our assumptions, and grow in ways that comfort and complacency never allow. Success may validate our efforts, but failure refines our character and resolve.

Thomas Edison famously said, "I have not failed. I've just found 10,000 ways that won't work." This mindset is what separates those who ultimately succeed from those who give up too soon. Edison's perseverance is a testament to the truth that each failure, rather than a dead end, is a stepping stone guiding us closer to our success.

Failure as a Catalyst for Innovation

Some of history's greatest breakthroughs were born from mistakes. The discovery of penicillin, the invention of the Post-it notes, and even the creation of microwave ovens were all accidental failures in one sense that opened the door to something greater. These moments remind us that rigid perfectionism can be a barrier to innovation, while a willingness to fail, adapt and learn can lead to unexpected brilliance. Failing fast is a theory of trying concepts, testing them repeatedly and then evaluating if the plan is working. If not, fail it/abandon it and try again.

The genius DaVinci believed that when trying to solve a problem, the name of the problem was listed in the middle of the page. From there in a circular fashion, he put potential solutions around the named problem. No potential solution was too outlandish, if it entered DaVinci's mind it went on the paper without judgement. This is how DaVinci invented the glider, the tank, the helicopter, and other inventions that only stayed on paper until hundreds of years later. Whole Person leaders think creatively like DaVinci. To be successful, you should think not only outside of the box, but outside of the house, outside of the city, outside of the country, and outside of the planet. If DaVinci had stayed within conventional wisdom, most of his amazing inventions would never have been invented or even thought of. When failure is seen as a necessary part of the creative process, individuals and organizations alike become more willing to take risks. And without risk, there can be no reward.

The Growth Mindset

Psychologist Carol Dweck introduced the concept of a "Growth Mindset," the belief that abilities and intelligence can be developed through effort, learning, and persistence. Those with a growth mindset see failure not as a reflection of their identity, but as a signal that growth is happening. This mindset transforms failure from something to be ashamed of into a necessary, even valuable, experience. When we embrace failure as a stepping stone, we begin to measure success not only by outcomes but also by resilience — the ability to rise after falling, again and again.

And again.

Resilience and Character

Success tests our skills. Failure tests our character. The path through failure is often difficult, marked by doubt, fear, and discomfort. But it is also the path that shapes grit, humility, and inner strength. These qualities, forged in adversity, are often what sustain success once it is achieved.

Many successful people credit their lowest moments with giving them the clarity and courage to change direction, to push harder, or to reimagine what was possible. In this way, failure does not just precede success—it sculpts the person who can hold it with grace.

The journey to success is rarely a straight line. It twists through valleys of disappointment, over hills of hard-won lessons, and across bridges built from perseverance. Each failure along the way adds a stone to that path—a necessary, even beautiful part of the process.

In the end, success is not the absence of failure but the mastery of it. Every person who has reached the summit once stood at the base, feet bloodied and spirit tested. And with each fall, they rose again—stronger, wiser, and more determined than ever to keep climbing.

Success is not achieved in spite of failure, but because of it. So be bold and try things without reservation.

Chapter 6.

Time is Your Greatest Asset

In the pursuit of success, people often think of money, talent, or connections as the primary ingredients. But one resource surpasses them all — time. It's the great equalizer. No matter who you are — a billionaire, a student, a single parent, or an entrepreneur just starting out — you get the same 24 hours in a day. What separates the successful from the stagnant is how they use that time.

Understanding the Value of Time

The richest people in the world don't have more hours in a day. They just treat each hour like it's a piece of gold. Time, unlike any other resource, is non-renewable. Once it's spent, it's gone — permanently. You can earn back money, rebuild relationships, or restart a project, but you will never get back lost time.

Think of your time as an investment portfolio. Every minute you spend is like spending a dollar. Would you casually throw money at meaningless distractions? If not, then why treat time any differently?

Time vs. Busyness

Many people confuse being busy with being productive. But busyness can be a form of laziness — lazy thinking and indiscriminate action. Success doesn't come from doing everything; it comes from doing the right things.

Every action you take is either a step toward your desired future or a distraction pulling you away from it. If something doesn't align with your objectives, it's likely working against them—even if subtly. There's a difference between living on autopilot and living on purpose. When you're constantly reacting to what life throws at you, you lose control of your direction. Intention allows you to choose your path deliberately.

Hope is not a strategy. And over time, aimless drifting can leave you feeling burned out, unfulfilled, and uncertain about where your time and energy have gone. Living life on purpose, by contrast, is about intention. It's about taking back the reins. When you live intentionally, you make conscious choices based on your values, your goals, and your long-term vision— not just what's urgent or expected. You decide what matters most and shape your days around that. You begin to experience clarity, alignment, and a greater sense of control—not because everything is easy, but because everything has meaning.

Purpose doesn't eliminate challenges, but it transforms how you face them. Instead of reacting blindly, you respond with awareness. Instead of being tossed around by life, you become the one charting your course.

Time Management Is Self-Management

Time is not just managed — it's directed. That direction comes from self-awareness and discipline. Want to see where your future is headed? Look at how you spend your average day. Success is built not in spurts of greatness, but in consistent, disciplined use of time over months and years.

Prioritization is everything. Learn to say no — not out of arrogance, but out of alignment with your purpose. If you don't protect your time, someone else will consume it for you.

Time Compounds Like Interest

Every small action you take today—every focused hour, every consistent habit, every intentional choice — may seem insignificant in the moment. But over days, weeks, and years, those moments multiply. They generate returns far greater than their face value.

The same way a small investment can grow into a fortune through the power of compound interest, the way you spend your time each day adds up to the life you're building. It's not the big, flashy sprints that create lasting success; it's the small, consistent deposits of effort, discipline, and focus.

This is why how you manage your time matters. It's not just about what you get done today — it's about what you're building long-term. Wasting time doesn't just cost you the moment; it robs you of the compounding value that time could've produced.

Treat time like an investment. Guard it. Use it with intention. Let it grow in value by choosing wisely again and again. The results won't come overnight, but they will come — and when they do, they'll be exponential.

Here's where time becomes your greatest asset and compounds:

- One hour a day reading turns into hundreds of hours of knowledge over a year.

- One focused hour a day on your side hustle could build a business.

- One deep conversation a week strengthens lifelong relationships.

Success rarely comes in a flash. It comes in layers, built brick by brick, over time. The more wisely you invest your hours, the greater the return. Like compound interest, it may not look like much today, but in a year — or ten — the difference is staggering.

Audit Your Time Ruthlessly.

Start keeping a time journal. Track how you actually spend your days for a week. You might be shocked at how much time bleeds away in trivial pursuits: scrolling social media, watching television, overcommitting, procrastinating.

Your time is your most valuable non-renewable resource — yet it's often spent carelessly, given away to distractions, obligations, and tasks that don't serve your highest priorities. To make meaningful progress toward your goals, you must be willing to look at how you're actually spending your time, not just how you think you are.

This means taking a hard, honest look at your days and asking: Where is my time really going? Track it. Write it down. Break it down by hour if you have to. Notice the patterns. How much time is going toward progress? How much is lost to procrastination, unnecessary scrolling, unproductive meetings, or saying "yes" to things you should've declined?

Auditing your time ruthlessly isn't about perfection — it's about awareness. When you know where your time is leaking, you can begin to seal those cracks. You can prioritize the tasks that matter, delegate or eliminate the ones that don't, and start living with greater focus and purpose.

Every goal you have — every dream, every breakthrough—is on the other side of how you manage your time. If you want your life to change, start by changing how you spend your hours. Don't wait until you're overwhelmed or behind. Audit now. Adjust now. The future you're building depends on it.

The Power of Moments

Don't fall into the trap of thinking success means grinding 24/7. Rest, reflection, and meaningful relationships are not time wasted — they're time invested. The point is not to fill every second with motion, but to be deliberate.

You don't need more time. You need to value the time you already have.

Time is the currency of life. Spend it on things that matter — your vision, your values, your legacy. The clock is ticking whether you use it or not, so use it on purpose. When you begin to see time not just as something to be managed but something to be mastered, you begin to see success not as a distant goal, but as a series of daily decisions.

And here's the truth: You already have what it takes — 24 hours a day. The only question is: what will you do with them?

Chapter 7.

There is No Growth Without Discomfort

Growth doesn't come wrapped in comfort. It doesn't knock politely at your door, asking if it's a good time. It often comes unannounced — disguised as a challenge, cloaked in failure, or hidden behind uncertainty. But here's the truth: discomfort is not the enemy; it's the evidence that you're stretching beyond what you were yesterday.

Discomfort Is the Doorway

We often romanticize success and transformation. We crave the outcomes—confidence, competence, strength, peace—but we flinch at the process. And yet, the process is where the growth lives. Learning something new means feeling awkward. Changing a habit means resisting old patterns. Healing means facing pain. Leading means carrying responsibility. In each case, discomfort is the doorway, not the wall.

Think about it: the muscle only grows after the strain. New ideas only emerge when old ones are challenged. Resilience doesn't come from having it easy — it comes from walking through hard seasons and still standing.

The Biology of Change

Even your brain agrees: growth is uncomfortable. When you try to learn a new skill or adopt a new behavior, your brain must break its old pathways and build new ones. That rewiring takes energy. It takes effort. It takes friction. That resistance you feel when you're doing something unfamiliar? It's biology's way of saying, "Something important is happening here."

Most people turn back at that point. But the brave ones —
those who understand that growth doesn't feel good at first —
they lean in.

Comfort Zones Are Shrinking Rooms

Comfort zones are deceiving. They feel safe, but they quietly
shrink over time. What once felt like a temporary reprieve
becomes a permanent prison. The longer you stay there, the
more your world narrows. Opportunities start to look like
threats. Challenges feel insurmountable. And eventually, you
forget what you were capable of.

To grow, you must be willing to feel a little out of place.
Growth never happens in the comfort of certainty or routine —
it begins at the edge of what feels familiar. It requires the
humility to admit you don't know everything, and the courage
to become a beginner again. This isn't weakness — it's
wisdom. The best leaders are lifelong learners, and learning
demands that we step into the unknown, ask better questions,
and be willing to be uncomfortable.

Discomfort is not a flaw in the process — it's proof that you're in motion. It's the friction that comes when your current self meets the demands of your future self. And while it's tempting to retreat back to what feels safe, the truth is that safety often disguises stagnation. To evolve into a better version of yourself — whether as a leader, a partner, or a human being — you must allow discomfort to stretch you rather than shrink you.

Being Teachable

There is power in being teachable. When you release the pressure to always have the answers, you make space for growth, innovation, and real connection. People trust leaders who are honest about what they're learning, not just what they know. So don't resist the feeling of being out of your depth. Embrace it. That tension you feel? It's the sign that you're alive. That awkwardness? It's evidence that something new is being built inside you.

As leaders grow in influence and experience, it becomes even more critical that they remain teachable. Success can create a dangerous illusion — that we've arrived, that we know enough, that we no longer need input. But the moment a leader stops learning is the moment they start falling behind.

Teachable leaders stay open. They seek feedback instead of avoiding it. They remain curious, not just about what's next, but about how they can improve, adapt, and lead more effectively. Being teachable doesn't mean lacking confidence — it means having the humility to recognize that growth is ongoing.

The best leaders are students first. They surround themselves with voices that challenge them, stretch them, and sharpen their thinking. They don't let their title or track record become a barrier to development.

In a world that's constantly evolving, a teachable spirit is not optional — it's essential.

Growth is not glamorous — but it is always worth it. And the leaders who are brave enough to be uncomfortable today are the ones most prepared to lead with wisdom tomorrow.

The Myth of Readiness

One of the most dangerous beliefs is that you must feel ready before you act. You won't. Growth doesn't wait for permission. It demands that you take the first step while your knees are still shaking.

Courage isn't the absence of fear—it's the decision that something else matters more. The person you want to become won't appear through wishing. They'll show up through repeated, uncomfortable choices. Saying no when it's easier to say yes. Starting when it's easier to stall. Speaking up when it's easier to stay silent.

Readiness is a moving target, and if you spend your life waiting for the perfect moment, you'll wait forever.

The truth is, most of the people doing great things didn't feel ready when they started. They stepped forward anyway — uncertain, imperfect, and often afraid. What they understood is that action creates clarity. Movement builds momentum. Confidence is not a prerequisite for progress — it's a byproduct of it.

Growth doesn't happen before the action — it happens through the action. You don't become a great leader, speaker, parent, or visionary by preparing endlessly. You become great by showing up, failing forward, and learning in motion.

If you're waiting to feel ready, you may be using it as a socially acceptable way to avoid fear. But fear is not the enemy — inaction is. Fear is a sign you're at the edge of something meaningful. And if you're willing to take one small step despite it, you prove to yourself that readiness was never the point — willingness was.

You don't need permission. You don't need more credentials. You don't need every detail figured out. You just need to GO.

Start messy. Show up imperfect. Trust that you'll learn what you need to know along the way.

Because at the end of the day, you become ready by beginning — not by waiting.

Reframing the Struggle

The question isn't, "How do I avoid discomfort?" The better question is, "What kind of discomfort is worth it?"

There's the discomfort of staying stuck — resenting your limits, questioning your potential, watching others live fully while you hesitate.

And there's the discomfort of progress — sore muscles, hard conversations, failed attempts, and small, invisible wins. Both are uncomfortable. One leads to regret. The other leads to growth.

Which pain would you rather live with?

Let Discomfort Be Your Teacher

Discomfort isn't here to punish you. It's here to shape you. Every time you stretch, you gain strength. Every time you fail, you gain insight. Every time you face what scares you, you reclaim a piece of your power.

So the next time you feel that knot in your stomach, that internal resistance, that voice saying, "This is hard," take a breath and smile. It means you're on the edge of greatness.

Greatness demands exploration. Innovation requires experimentation. And transformation only happens when you're willing to step beyond what's comfortable, predictable, and safe. That means trying things that might not work. Thinking thoughts you've never thought before. Challenging long-held assumptions — even the ones that have gotten you

The comfort zone is where potential goes to sleep.

this far. You have to open your mind before you can open new doors.

The comfort zone is where routine replaces curiosity, and where fear is disguised as logic. Leaders who stay there may avoid failure — but they also avoid growth, and they avoid the kind of discovery that leads to their next level.

When you start experimenting beyond your usual methods — when you take creative risks, engage with different perspectives, or lead in a new way — you shake off the limits you didn't even realize were holding you back. You realize that the box wasn't just keeping you safe — it was keeping you small.

That's why every major breakthrough has discomfort in its DNA. Every reward is preceded by risk. And every great leader has had a moment where they chose to step out before they were certain.

The prize doesn't show up for those who wait inside the lines. It reveals itself to those bold enough to color outside of them. So open your mind. Step out of the box. And don't just think differently—live differently.

Chapter 8.

Relational Banking

In accounting, every action has a counterpart: a debit must be matched with a credit. Balance is not optional — it is essential. While this principle is foundational in finance, it holds a deeper resonance in the realm of human relationships. Every word spoken, every favor granted, every act of trust or betrayal— these are all, in a way, emotional transactions.

By reimagining human relationships through the lens of debits and credits, we gain insight into how we build, maintain, and sometimes lose connection with others. In this chapter, we explore how the emotional ledgers we keep — consciously or unconsciously — govern the dynamics of trust, respect, and reciprocity.

The Emotional Ledger

Just as companies maintain financial ledgers to track value exchanged, humans maintain emotional ledgers — subtle records of interactions and impacts. These ledgers influence how safe we feel, how much we trust, and how deeply we're willing to connect. Over time, they shape the emotional credit or debt we carry in our relationships, whether we realize it or not.

Emotional Debits

An emotional debit draws on the relationship. It may include:

- Asking for help without reciprocating

- Breaking trust

- Failing to acknowledge someone's effort

- Withholding empathy or support

Emotional Credits

An emotional credit adds to the relationship. Examples include:

- Acts of kindness

- Listening deeply

- Offering encouragement or praise

- Following through on promises

Like in accounting, no relationship can survive in perpetual deficit. Debits must be balanced with credits — if not numerically, then emotionally.

You need to have a positive balance in your relationship bank in order to make withdrawals.

Just like in finance, relationships operate on deposits and withdrawals. Every act of kindness, every moment of active listening, every gesture of support—those are deposits. They build trust, emotional safety, and goodwill. And just like a real bank account, the more consistent the deposits, the healthier the relationship becomes.

But there will be times when you need to make a withdrawal — when you have to deliver hard feedback, ask for grace, lean on someone during a crisis, or make a tough decision that impacts others. If the balance isn't there — if you haven't been investing regularly — those moments can cause strain, resentment, or even a breakdown in the relationship.

Leaders especially must understand this. Authority may give you a title, but trust gives you influence. And trust is earned over time through intentional deposits: showing up, being consistent, communicating clearly, and caring deeply.

The healthiest relationships — professional and personal — are built by people who understand that you can't just take. You must give, often and sincerely. You have to nurture the connection before you can rely on it.

So the next time you're about to make a withdrawal, pause and ask yourself: Have I made enough deposits to sustain this ask?

Double-Entry Humanity

The principle of double-entry bookkeeping — every entry must affect two accounts — is a powerful metaphor for relational ethics.

When we hurt someone, we not only debit their trust account; we also debit our own integrity. When we uplift someone, we credit their well-being and our own humanity.

Relational Example:

- You mentor a colleague (credit to their growth).

- You feel more fulfilled and respected (credit to your own sense of purpose).

True connection happens when our debits and credits reflect mutual benefit, growth, and accountability.

Relational Equity and Imbalance

In finance, equity is what remains after debts are paid — your true stake in the business. In relationships, equity could be seen as the emotional capital you build with someone over time.

When one person continually deposits (emotional credits) and another only withdraws (emotional debits), imbalance occurs. Eventually, the account runs dry.

This leads to:

- Burnout

- Resentment

- Withdrawal

Healthy relationships, like healthy accounts, require regular deposits. Trust and love are not guaranteed — they are accumulated over time, through consistent action and intention.

Interest and Compounding

Financial interest rewards investment over time. The same is true emotionally.

Small, consistent relational credits — like remembering a birthday, checking in during tough times, or giving honest praise — can compound into deep, lasting bonds. Conversely, small neglects may accrue unnoticed until the relationship is bankrupt.

Key Idea: In both money and love, what you invest regularly matters more than what you do occasionally.

What strengthens relationships is the daily efforts: showing up, listening, encouraging, apologizing, forgiving, and caring — over and over again. These are the small but steady deposits that build a relationship that can weather storms.

Whether you're nurturing your finances or your closest connections, remember: it's not about the big moments — it's about the regular ones. The quiet, consistent investments compound into trust, security, and enduring loyalty.

Write-Offs and Reconciliation

Sometimes, debts are uncollectible. We write them off and move on. The same applies to emotional harm.

Forgiveness, in this sense, is a conscious write-off. It doesn't mean the harm didn't happen, but that we're no longer investing energy in collecting repayment. It is an act of release, not denial. Reconciliation, meanwhile, is a rebalancing process. Like financial reconciliation, it involves:

- Transparency

- Acknowledgment of errors

- Recommitment to honest interaction

Building a Relationship Balance Sheet

Every relationship has its own "balance sheet" composed of:

- Assets: Shared memories, mutual respect, trust

- Liabilities: Unresolved issues, past harms, unspoken resentments

- Equity: The real strength of the bond — what remains when you subtract the liabilities from the assets

Just like in business, the goal is not perfection, but sustainability. You can't eliminate all liabilities — but you can grow your assets faster and manage your emotional expenses more wisely.

The Ethics of Relational Accounting

In finance, cooking the books is fraud. In relationships, so is pretending to give without sincerity, or demanding what you haven't earned.

Unethical relational accounting includes:

- Manipulating others into giving more

- Hiding emotional debts

- Expecting loyalty without reciprocity

Healthy relational accounting includes:

- Taking ownership of your emotional impact

- Communicating expectations

- Apologizing when you've overdrawn

Authentic relationships require honest books — clear ledgers of respect, care, and mutual investment.

Human relationships are not transactions in a cold, mechanical sense — but they do follow patterns of give and take, cause and effect, investment and return. By viewing our connections through the metaphor of debits and credits, we are invited to think more consciously about the balance we bring to each interaction.

To live well among others, we must track not only what we take, but what we give. And in doing so, we build relational wealth — measured not in dollars, but in trust, love, and devotion. Understanding the relational debits, credits and equity are essential for the whole person leader. It is critical to understand *you must overfund relationships in order to maximize performance in business.*

We must pay close attention not only to what we take from our relationships, but also to what we give. Just as we track deposits and withdrawals in a financial account, our relationships also carry balances—built on trust, maintained through consistency, and depleted by neglect or selfishness. Every interaction is a small investment, and over time, these moments accumulate to form what can only be described as relational wealth — a kind of intangible currency measured not in dollars, but in dedication.

For the Whole Person Leader, understanding the dynamics of relational debits, credits, and equity is essential. A careless word, a missed commitment, or a lack of empathy may seem small in isolation, but over time they subtract from your relational capital. On the other hand, acts of kindness, thoughtful listening, and sincere encouragement are powerful deposits. They build equity. They strengthen bonds. And they create a foundation of loyalty and goodwill that no performance incentive can replicate.

Leadership is not just about strategies, systems, or skill sets. It's about people. And people perform best when they feel valued, seen, and supported. This is why leaders must learn to overfund relationships — not as a tactic, but as a way of being. When we invest more than is expected — more attention, more grace, more consistency — we earn more than we can measure. The return on relational investment is long-term commitment, resilient culture, and inspired performance.

If you want to maximize results in business, you must first maximize trust. And trust is never built on empty leadership — it's built by leaders who understand that the most powerful influence begins with how you treat people when there's nothing to gain.

Chapter 9.

Training for Life Success

Success in life is rarely the result of luck alone. While external circumstances play a role, long-term success is most often cultivated through deliberate training—mental, emotional, physical, and tactical. Just like an athlete conditions their body for peak performance, those who thrive in life condition their habits, mindsets, and skills for resilience, clarity, and growth. This chapter explores how to train yourself for life success— not by chasing external validation, but by becoming the kind of person who naturally attracts and creates opportunity.

Define What Success Means to You

Before training begins, you must define your destination. Too often, people pursue a version of success they inherited—from parents, peers, or culture—without questioning whether it truly aligns with their values.

Success is not a fixed destination—it evolves as you grow. Keep refining your vision, and make sure it reflects you, not someone else's expectations. Successful leaders are always working toward a goal. When one is accomplished, another begins.

Develop Core Life Skills

Training for life success isn't just about mastering one field. It's about becoming adaptable, capable, resourceful and self-directed. There are several "core competencies" that successful people consistently work on:

- Emotional Regulation: The ability to stay calm under pressure and respond instead of react.

- Effective Communication: Whether you're speaking, writing, or listening, your ability to clearly express and understand ideas is crucial.

- Critical Thinking and Decision Making: Life is full of uncertainty. Learn to assess risks, ask the right questions, and make smart decisions.

- Time Management: Mastering your schedule is mastering your life. Prioritize what truly matters.

- Financial Literacy: Success is unsustainable without financial awareness. Learn how money works.

- Be caring, curious and committed to those that you lead.

- Humility—practice genuine humility

None of these skills are innate. They can all be trained with consistent practice, but you must be intentional. Remember, live every day on purpose.

Train Your Mind Daily

A strong mindset is the foundation of all success. But mental strength isn't about being "positive" all the time — it's about being grounded, focused, and able to endure setbacks. I call this *mental fortitude*.

It's the quiet discipline to stay aligned with your values and goals, regardless of distractions or pressure. It's the ability to think clearly, act intentionally, and maintain emotional balance — not because everything is perfect, but because you've trained yourself to lead with purpose.

Mental fortitude is what allows you to show up consistently, make thoughtful decisions, and remain composed when others may be reactive. It's built through habits of clarity, self-awareness, and emotional regulation. You don't need to force positivity or pretend to have all the answers — what matters is showing up with presence and inner strength.

This kind of mindset isn't flashy, but it's powerful. It creates space for growth, deep focus, and real leadership. It's not about having an edge only when things are hard — it's about carrying strength and intention into everything you do.

Surround Yourself with Growth

No one succeeds in isolation. The people around you shape your standards, influence your energy, and reflect what you believe is possible.

Leaders seek out mentors to help them grow and gain perspective. Leaders are also mentors to others. They understand that no matter how much experience or success they've achieved, there's always more to learn. A mentor offers insight, clarity, and the kind of wisdom that only comes from having walked the road ahead. Through mentorship, leaders sharpen their thinking, challenge blind spots, and stay aligned with their greater purpose.

But leadership isn't just about receiving guidance — it's also about offering it. Great leaders become mentors to others, intentionally investing in the growth of their teams, peers, and future leaders. They pass along lessons learned, model integrity, and create space for others to rise.

This dual role — being both student and teacher — is what sustains a culture of growth. It keeps leaders humble, open, and connected. And it ensures that the next generation doesn't start from scratch, but builds from a higher foundation.

True leadership is not a solo pursuit. It's a cycle of learning and lifting — seeking wisdom while sharing it forward.

Build Habits, Not Hype

Motivation fades. Discipline and habits endure. Your body was designed to be in motion. To train physically and mentally you must do things consistently. Consistency is the key. Success happens with consistent action. Failure happens with the inconsistent start/stop that most people do.

High performers don't rely on willpower; they rely on systemic habits. Habits create momentum — and momentum creates results. The key is the consistency of action.

True leadership isn't just built on mastering a single field — it's forged through adaptability, capability, resourcefulness, and self-direction. In a world that refuses to stand still, the most impactful leaders aren't the ones who know everything — they're the ones who can grow through anything.

Adaptable leaders rise when circumstances shift. They don't fear change — they harness it. Capable leaders go beyond titles and skillsets; they bring vision, clarity, and calm in the face of complexity. Resourceful leaders find a way forward, even when the path isn't clear. They turn constraints into creativity and setbacks into momentum. And self-directed leaders don't wait to be told what's possible — they pursue purpose with discipline, resilience, and a relentless commitment to growth.

Mastery might open the door, but it's adaptability that keeps it open. The leaders who shape the future are the ones who keep learning, keep moving, and keep showing others the way forward—not just with knowledge, but with courage and character.

Fail Forward

Earlier we talked about how Success is built on the stepping stones of failure. Failure is miscategorized as the absence of success, but as you learned that is far from the truth. Success isn't about never failing — it's about not letting failure stop you. Remember failure is essential to success. Every successful person has faced rejection, embarrassment, and defeat. What sets them apart is how they interpret and respond to setbacks. They welcome failure because it is such a powerful teacher.

In the 28 years before becoming President, Abraham Lincoln failed at so many things, including losing eight elections, failing in business, and having a nervous breakdown. After so many setbacks that would have paralyzed a lesser man, Abraham Lincoln saw them as teachable moments that allowed him to become one of the greatest presidents in our history. His failures were the stepping stones to his eventual success.

Wayne Gretzky, referred to in hockey as 'The Great One', said he missed every shot he didn't take. Michael Jordan did make the high school team as a sophomore, instead of looking at it as a rejection, he spent the next year refining his skills, getting stronger, getting faster. He came back to not only make the team but then go on to earn a scholarship to UNC where he would lead them to a college basketball championship, later becoming the greatest NBA basketball player of all time.

Failure is your greatest teacher and will be the catalyst to your success.

Keep Your Integrity

In the pursuit of success, don't lose yourself. Remember integrity is a core element of the ACE principle. Integrity and Character are synonymous terms. Integrity is the anchor that keeps you from drifting away from your values. Without it, any success will feel hollow and meaningless. Have you ever met someone that is very successful, but also absolutely miserable? This is because they sacrificed their integrity for the pursuit of success. This is like drinking salt water when you are thirsty. It is a losing proposition.

Training for life success is not a one-time event. It's a lifelong commitment to growth, learning, and self-mastery. There's no "finish line"— just higher levels of challenge and purpose.

Begin with where you are. Build one habit at a time. Invest in your mindset, skills, and character. Over time, you'll become the kind of person who not only achieves success — but sustains it with meaning and impact.

Key Takeaways:

- Success must be defined personally to be meaningful.

- Core life skills are trainable and foundational.

- Mindset is a muscle—train it daily.

- Habits are the engine of progress.

- Failure is not the enemy; stagnation is.

- Success built on values endures longer than success built on image.

You are in training. Every day is a rep. Keep going.

Chapter 10.

Tying it All Together

Being a Whole Person Leader is not a destination — it's a full-life pursuit. It's the kind of leadership that doesn't clock out, doesn't compartmentalize, and certainly doesn't hide behind titles or appearances. It demands everything of you — your physical stamina, mental clarity, emotional presence, and relational awareness. And yet, it returns even more.

At its core, Whole Person leadership is about being fully human while helping others become the best version of themselves. It's about embracing the weight of influence with humility, curiosity, and commitment. It is about living life on purpose and being intentional about every pursuit. It is about creating a culture that attracts and keeps people. It is about leading people through all of life's ups and downs. The goal is not power. It's not control. The goal is connection — deep, authentic, and enduring. The goal is to be the kind of leader people want to follow.

The Heart of Leadership: Love and Respect

If you want people to follow you — not because they 'have to', but because they want to — you must become the kind of leader worthy of their loyalty. The kind they'd run through a brick wall for, not out of blind obedience, but out of love, respect, and shared belief in something greater than themselves.

But that kind of loyalty can't be demanded. It must be earned. Daily. Quietly. Authentically.

People don't follow titles — they follow people. And they don't admire you because you're the smartest or the most skilled. They admire you because of who you are, how you show up, and how you make them feel. You don't need to know all the answers, but you do need to listen like they matter. You don't need to fix every problem, but you do need to stand beside people in their challenges and help them believe they can overcome with you alongside. It is like running a three-legged race. They need to know you are all in.

The Three Pillars: Attitude, Character, and Effort

True leadership rests on the three pillars of ACE. Everything else — skills, connections, intelligence — is secondary.

- **Attitude** is your emotional posture toward adversity and opportunity. It's how you carry yourself in the storm and how you treat others when things get tough.

- **Character** is who you are when no one is watching. It's the alignment between what you say and what you do. It's integrity in motion.

- **Effort** is the relentless pursuit of better—for yourself, for your people, and for your mission. It's about showing up every day, not just when it's easy or convenient.

These traits are not innate gifts; they are choices. And when you choose them consistently, you become the kind of person others want to follow. It is from the foundation of ACE that you will build your leadership house.

Leadership as Service

Whole Person leadership is not about authority — it's about service. It's about waking up each day and asking, "How can I help someone else succeed today?" It's about seeing leadership not as a platform for self-promotion but as an opportunity to elevate others. It is about seeing the greatness in someone else and drawing it out. When Michelangelo carved his masterpiece, 'La Pieta', he commissioned a single cube of marble. What makes this statue truly remarkable is that for the first time in history, the arms of the figures were a part of the stone. Meaning they were not carved separately and then attached. When Michelangelo was asked about this masterpiece, he said. "I simply drew the Virgin Mary and the Christ out of the rock. I simply removed what didn't need to be there." The master saw the masterpiece in the rock. Everyone you lead is a masterpiece waiting to be revealed.

You lead best when you meet people where they are, not where you wish they were. That means taking time to understand their fears, dreams, motivations, and struggles. It means having the courage to speak truth in love, to challenge when necessary, and to encourage when they doubt themselves. It means to constantly be looking for opportunities to praise and celebrate.

Whether someone is at their peak or in their lowest valley, a Whole Person leader walks alongside them — present, honest, and fully engaged.

Becoming, Not Arriving

This journey isn't clean or linear. You won't always get it right. But leadership isn't about perfection — it's about progress. It's about becoming, not arriving. Every conversation, every decision, every moment is an opportunity to either build trust or break it.

Reflection

Ask yourself:

• Are you the kind of leader you would follow?

• Are you living in a way that inspires others to do the same?

• Are you helping others become more whole by the way

you lead?

If you're ready to dive deeper into these principles and put

them into practice, there is a companion workbook available.

The Whole Person Leader: Workbook by David Hatzfeld.

Conclusion

Being a Whole Person Leader is a lifelong pursuit. It's not a job description — it's a way of living. It requires daily commitment to growth in every area of life: physically, mentally, emotionally, and relationally. It means showing up with care, curiosity, and consistency, no matter the setting or the stakes.

True leadership isn't about authority — it's about service. It's about being the kind of person others want to follow because of how you live, how you lead, and how you treat people when no one's watching.

If you want people to respect and trust you — so much so that they'd stand beside you through challenges and victories alike — you must become the kind of leader who earns that respect through action, not words. Leadership is never about perfection. It's about being intentional, being human, and being present.

Skills can be taught. Intelligence can be sharpened. But Attitude, Character, and Effort — these are the foundations of real influence. And when you lead with those at the forefront, you become the kind of leader who leaves a lasting mark.

A Whole Person Leader creates more than momentum — they create transformation. And their greatest impact will always be the people who became whole, confident, and capable because they led with purpose.

About the Author

David Hatzfeld is a lifelong learner, seasoned entrepreneur, and dynamic leader with a passion for both business and people development. Holding a double major in Economics and Political Science, along with double minors in French Literature and Art History, David brings a uniquely well-rounded perspective to leadership and personal growth.

Over the course of his career, David has built, owned, and successfully sold multiple businesses, gaining firsthand insight into the challenges and rewards of entrepreneurship. Beyond the boardroom, he has coached both sports teams and sales teams, combining strategy with motivation to help individuals reach their highest potential.

Whether mentoring rising leaders or guiding teams through change, David is driven by a deep belief in the power of intentional leadership—and in the transformation that happens when people are challenged to grow beyond what they thought was possible.